ERIC FREEMAN

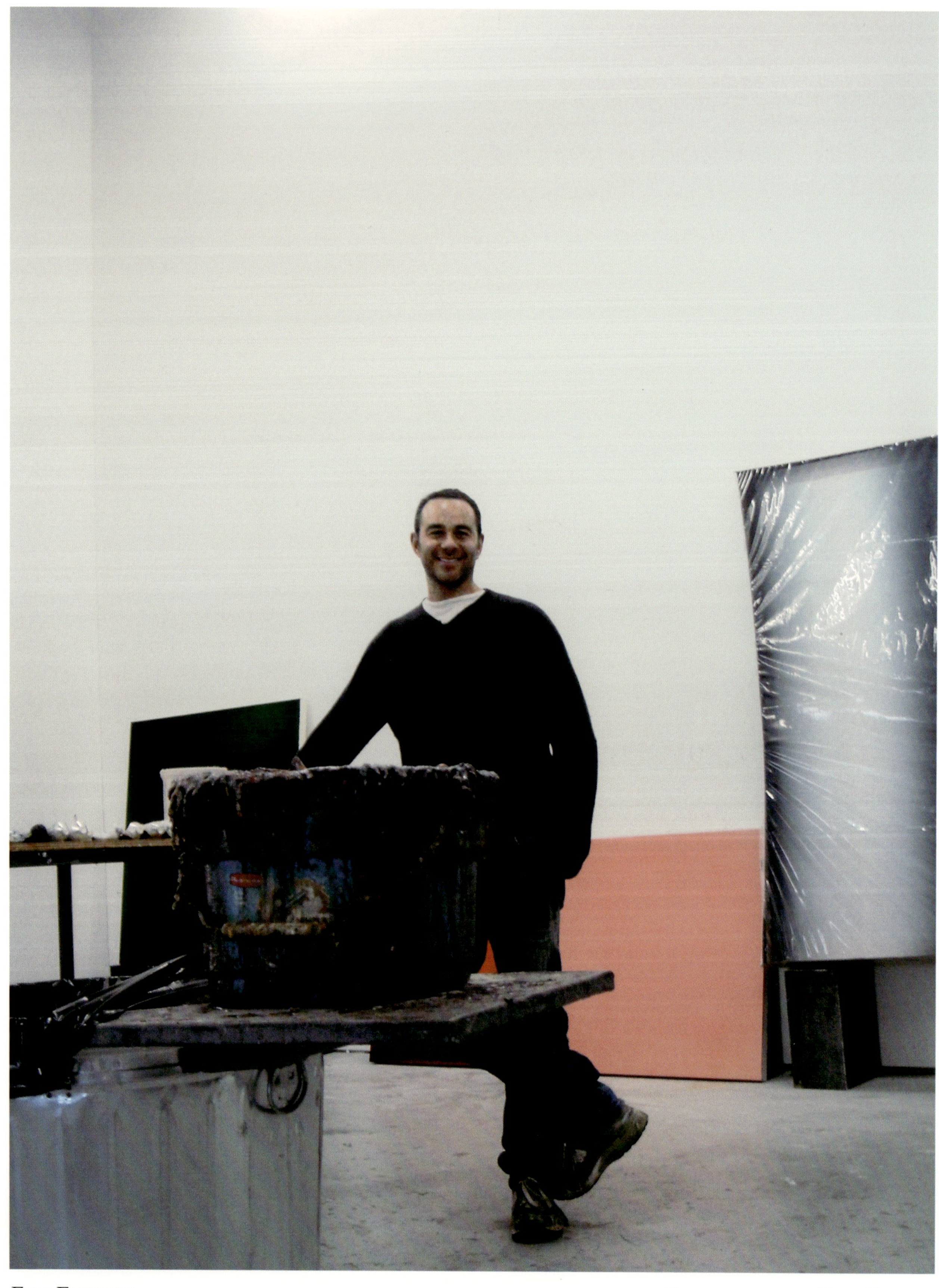

Eric Freeman

ERIC FREEMAN

GALLERY ALAIN NOIRHOMME

RUE DE LA RÉGENCE 17 REGENTSCHAPSSTRAAT

BRUSSELS

INTERVIEW BETWEEN

ERIC FREEMAN AND CALVIN KLEIN

Eric Freeman: Do you have any interest in contemporary objects?

Calvin Klein: Well, I like to live in a contemporary world. I'm certainly not a traditionalist. I've always liked, whether it's clothes, fashion, or architecture, or interior design. I just recently started to get into furniture from the 16th and 17th centuries. That's a whole new experience for me, because I have always leaned toward very simple contemporary shapes. I still don't see myself collecting contemporary art, even though I have respect for a lot of the artists.

EF: Well, you have an interest in a few, like Rothko.

CK: I don't consider him contemporary. If he is, maybe it's because he's abstract, and it certainly is about the simple but very complicated way he paints.

EF: Have you ever been influenced by any of these artists?

CK: By Rothko, in particular, because I work with color all the time. And we are constantly having to come up with color combinations, and I've always been passionate about his colors. I mean always. It's come through in collection after collection. I'm always bringing in reproductions of Rothko's works into the design studio, and saying let's get started with his colors. You know, because we work with patterns and prints. We often let ourselves be inspired by artists.

EF: Who are themselves the outcome of inspiration. In my paintings I refer to sculpture and space a lot. Recently I have been inspired by the work of James Turrell – his light and space and sense of architecture. That sense of the three-dimensional, which you spoke of earlier, it's in Turrell, and I try to achieve that same feeling now with these new paintings. I hope that's coming across.

CK: Well, everyone sees things from their own perspective.

EF: Remember that day we went to see the Richard Serra show at the Museum of Modern Art?

CK: Yes.

EF: That show, when we walked through it, really got me going It influenced the direction of my most recent paintings. I have been kind of working off of that sensation of space. Even the new studio that I made deals with the same concepts of space and architecture.

CK: Richard Serra is another one – I mean I could live with his work. And, I don't know what that's about, but maybe it's also the material — half of my apartment is made of steel. So, whether it's inside or outside, I like form and shape, and that it be three-dimensional.

EF: The materials he uses are so beautiful, so natural…

CK: And what's beautiful also is to see what happens to them…

EF: Over time.

CK: As they age. That's very special.

EF: Whenever I think of what a sculpture should be or look like, Serra comes to mind. Even if I think of Brancusi, too; but mostly it's Serra, as

7

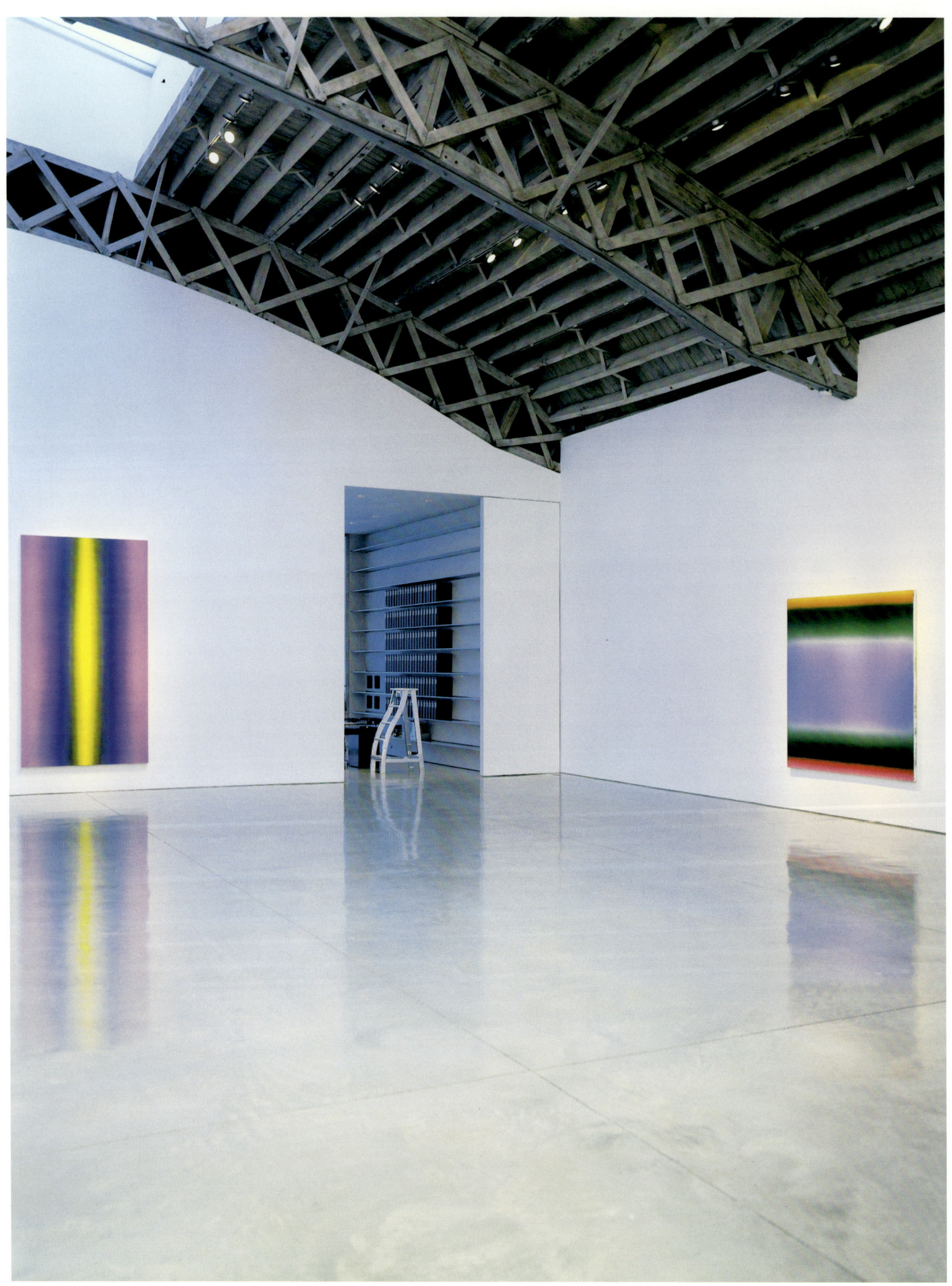

Eric Freeman at Mary Boone Gallery, New York, 2005

far as what I feel contemporary sculpture is all about, and this is also because his work approaches the sublime — not to use a cliché — and because this is what I believe art can still aspire to.

CK: At the same time, we were talking about Warhol. You know he had without a doubt a huge impact on the contemporary world — and not just on the art part of it It's so interesting because I don't think anyone who knew him had any idea that would happen. That it would be anything like what it has become. Not that there weren't people who collected his work at the beginning. But most people were just interested in having their portraits done, and, of course, he was interested in the money. But it's his other paintings that captured a moment in time, and that has had an amazing impact on the world.

EF: Even if his work represents the antithesis of the other work we have been talking about…

CK: But we can't limit his impact to the soup cans. That just didn't interest me. There were so many other kinds of work…

EF: I understand.

CK: Brancusi interests me. And we were talking about Rothko. What interests me there is that it changes so much. Every time you look at it, even the way the paint is laid down seems to change.

EF: In a way, Andy's work is that way, too.

CK: While personally I could live without many kinds of art, I am always discovering something new in these artists' work.

EF: Do you think your association with pop culture has influenced you — because you are more like an arbiter of pop culture yourself? And maybe he was kind of fascinated by what you do…

CK: Did I ever tell you he did a thing with my underwear? On canvas.

EF: Really. I guess he was interested in the advertising dimension of it. What did he do with it?

CK: He attached underwear to a canvas and did some scribbling, and then put it in a plastic box and sent it to me.

EF: What did you do with it?

CK: I don't know. I remember getting it, but I don't know what happened to it. I didn't pay too much attention to it at the time.

EF: Well, it's definitely not on the wall.

CK: Kelly has some of the Christmas cards.

EF: Oh, those little ones.

CK: Kelly has those. Those were cute.

EF: You told me once that Warhol did a show of Dan Flavin at your store.

CK: It wasn't a show. It was Christmas windows, and it was the last thing he did before he died. And, at that time, we were trying to think of artists that I didn't know — so that it wouldn't hurt us too much if they turned us down. You just never know. We are a store on Madison Avenue and many artists wouldn't want to be associated with that kind of thing. But, I think Dan Flavin was really interesting. When he did it — others did it as well, but he really stood out as the best.

EF: I'm sure it was the perfect kind of space for that work.

CK: His work relates so much to architecture — and he used it in a wonderful way. But somehow we always touch on the art world or being influenced by it.

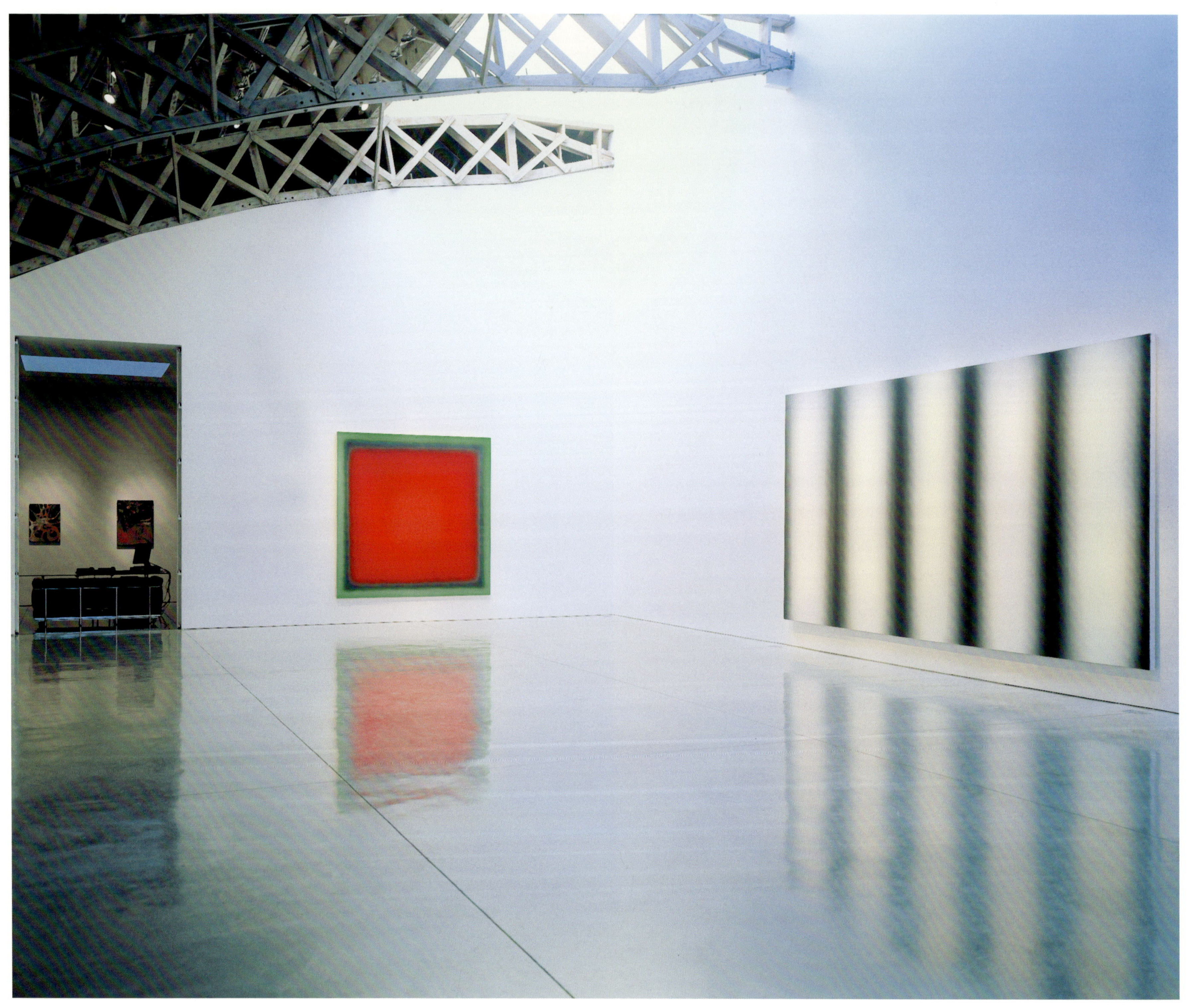

Eric Freeman at Mary Boone Gallery, New York, 2005

EF: Have you been to Marfa?

CK: That's how I really got into appreciating Donald Judd. That is such a spiritual experience, to be in that space inside his home. The surrounding area — those concrete boxes that are out in the fields, or the steel boxes that are in what was once a hangar... There's nothing quite like it — that really kind of changes your life in a certain way, and that was a big change for me. I suddenly wanted to live the way Judd lived. In fact, I have bought things from the foundation for the store.

EF: I think the place the artist works influences or is a factor in the work he produces. People say that artists can work wherever they want, but I find that I can't do that. The place where I work is very critical to my production. Marfa speaks to that idea, because he had all that open space.

CK: He needed that space. You can't show, much less create, that kind of work without such space. To really see those pieces at their best, you need acres. It's too massive and he knew that. The land there costs nothing. It's totally flat and away from any civilization. It's interesting, what Judd also did in town, because he had offices where he would work, and so he renovated some of the buildings.

EF: Oh, really?

CK: And he also collected furniture. He had a lot of his own furniture — daybeds, desks, tables. But he also had a collection of chairs by others — pieces that were soft — furniture that you would recognize — Aalto, for instance. And, the way he treated the walls at the entrances to the rooms…it was different than what I think of Judd. These were old buildings and they were his very particular renovations.

EF: He was sensitive to what they were. I think this goes back to things being natural — finding beauty in what's natural. Instead of trying to change the building, he often just brought the natural elements out of the materials.

CK: He did that and respected the architecture — through paint, through trimmings, doors. He did something to accentuate what was already wonderful about it. And still it was what it was. He didn't change much, but you could see his touch. I remember there was a bank in Marfa that he had worked on — some of the buildings were crumbling — he would leave some of that and then restore other parts of it.

EF: It looked like a wedding chapel in an old building. He left the walls but the roof was missing.

CK: I also went to visit Georgia O'Keeffe in Santa Fe, and she let Bruce Weber photograph me at the Ghost Ranch, which was also amazing.

EF: Were you interested in her painting?

CK: I loved her work — the colors she used. I owned a few O'Keeffe paintings at the time. It is always interesting to see how these people lived, because with O'Keeffe you could feel the environment she lived in inside the paintings. Somehow there was a real relationship with Judd. I am thinking of one room where the ground, the floor, is an abstraction — where he was able to do that with cement and rocks.

EF: I know that room.

CK: It really blows your mind. You can't believe it.

EF: I think artists are very much in tune with their surroundings and the places where they live. I guess that's why it seems so natural that they get into making furniture. Furniture expresses the way you live in your environment. I have become interested in making some myself.

CK: There are stories about why he created those daybeds all over the place. They say that at certain times during the day Judd would pass out, so wherever he ended up, that is where he would fall asleep. So, everywhere you went there was a bed.

EF: Sounds nice to me.

CK: I've always thought architects make some pretty amazing furniture — furniture that I always wind up liking — and they usually make it when they don't have a job doing buildings.

EF: Furniture by architects always seems less interesting in its functionality, but more interesting in its design; when artists make furniture, it is much more pragmatic.

CK: I'm trying to think of what would be the difference. The only thing I see in Judd's furniture is that there is his art in it. Because it was so much like his work, it became sculpture. It certainly wasn't about comfort.

EF: That's true.

CK: You know there are great architects who struggle to achieve a certain beauty and shape. But he simply looked at it in very strict, very pure terms.

EF: Straight and square. No handles on the back.

CK: No curves. Very strict, like his work. To me, that was very exciting. You could have it on a large scale in the middle of the room and it doesn't have to go on the wall.

EF: You don't like anything on the walls…

CK: No. In fact, in the apartment that John Pawson just did for me in the Richard Meier building there are almost no walls. It's all black. It's all about the view.

EF: You don't have that much hanging on the walls out here — maybe two things.

CK: This gets back to Joe Derso again. Joe got me into leaning things. Putting them on the floor and just leaning them against the wall rather than hanging them. And stacking them, too.

EF: I think that it's an interesting aesthetic.

CK: But I also like going to people's homes who have walls entirely covered with photographs. I like that. I just don't do it myself.

EF: It seems to me that in the contemporary art world beauty is looked down upon as being basically vapid. I feel that something can be intellectual and beautiful at the same time. It doesn't have to be shocking or ugly to have intellectual value.

CK: In the fashion world, it is all we think about. Some designers — but that's a whole other thing — have clothes no one wants to wear because they don't make you look good. They are just dreadful. They are clothes to be studied, not worn.

EF: In a way, that's like furniture when it becomes sculpture.

CK: This kind of design has everything in mind except what a woman wants to wear. Certain Japanese designers get very intellectual. But there are women who like to hide their bodies. Most European and American women don't. They work very hard in the gymnasiums, running, doing their thing to stay in shape. They want to show off their bodies. This kind of approach is more in your face, more obvious. We try to achieve beauty that is related to the body, but there is a fine line. In my work, we were always concerned with being beautiful and sexy, not trashy. Because it's easy to create clothes or to create objects or environments that are not attractive, that are not fine. What many designers try to do is something that is beautiful and sensual at the same time.

EF: So, when you go to a museum, what do you look for? Is it beauty per se or something less definable?

CK: I don't think about painting or art in terms of whether it is or isn't beautiful. It doesn't occur to me in that way. When the Met had a show of Matisse paintings, they also showed the fabrics he had collected and how he used them and talked about them. To me, that was fascinating. I remember the Matisse/Picasso show and seeing the relationship between the two and wondering, who came first, in terms of a particular movement. That was pretty amazing. But, I didn't look at it in terms of whether it was beautiful or not. More like is it exciting? Does it do something to me emotionally?

EF: I think there is something so personal about work like that, like those Matisse cutouts.

CK: But don't you think everyone we have talked about — even Judd, Flavin and Turrell — that their work is an extension of themselves?

EF: There's nothing in between them and the work.

CK: I think that's true of any artist.

EF: Any good artist.

CK: A designer, an architect, anyone in any profession. It's the same. The work is an extension of who you are. At least, if it's going to matter. Their craft is an extension of everything they've learned.

EF: It's so rare, but I think that it is only the really good artists who can translate their feelings into a clear work of art.

CK: When I think of an artist, I never think in terms of a good artist. Because who's to judge what's good. I think sometimes young artists can't translate everything they would like to into their work because they don't have the skills yet.

EF: I think that what makes a good artist is the ability to look at your own work, to hone in on it and articulate it. Really good art reflects this ability.

CK: I call it editing. In fashion, we create a lot of things, and then we decide what we will present to the world. Suddenly I become a different person than the one who is creating. It's not that I'm not in love with everything I create, but I begin to see when I am looking critically that I love some things more than others. That's the editor side of me coming out, who becomes highly critical of what I've done. I'm a good editor.

EF: Then, obviously, in the past, you must have let some things into the world that you probably shouldn't have…you can't always get it right.

CK: You can, most of the time — whatever I have shown or put into a collection, whether home furnishings, fashion accessories, I have to like it. But it doesn't mean I love it the most. I suppose it's true…sometimes I look back and say how could I have ever liked that. But at the time, I did.

EF: Time is also a factor. Sometimes I struggle with the fact that something is out there that I wish wasn't. And there is another part of me trying to let it go and not obsess about it. I'm sure that it is something all creative people have to deal with in some way or other.

CK: Once I've done it, I'm over it.

EF: You have to get control, anyway.

CK: Exactly, what's the point in thinking about work that you've done and that's in the past? It's best to concentrate on the work you are doing now and what you might want to do in the future based on what you know, how you feel, and what your experiences are now. That, to me, is much more valuable than paying any attention to what you've already done and agonizing over it.

EF: Where do you find your inspiration?

CK: When I first started traveling, I would take little chips of paint off buildings for color, because I would see something I liked, especially in Italy. I would often be inspired by museum shows, an artist's work.

EF: Do you go to a lot of museums?

CK: I do, but I often don't see everything. I like to see what's going on. It could be a photographer or an architect's work. I've always liked to travel and go to museums. A trip to India was my first — everywhere I looked I could see St. Laurent. I could see where he got his influences — the way these women put colors together with their saris. Even their skin color had an impact. That was what St. Laurent did throughout his whole career. I was busy buying saris everywhere I could find them. And seeing stacks of amazing colors. I have all of those fabrics — luminous, because of the vegetable dyes they used. I brought them into different studios for people to work on, the way Matisse did, even though he was more often looking for patterns. But, I have lots of patterns, too. I found antique saris that were valuable because of their beauty, and because of the gold and silver threads. They were a source of direct inspiration. Sometimes an art book done in conjunction with a show could become a source of inspiration. That happened

Eric Freeman at Western-Project, Los Angeles, 2007

more than once with Rothko. We would look through the book for colors or for a transparency to layer with color.

EF: I can see how much you enjoyed this part of the process.

CK: I loved it. I used to go around the world searching for just the right color. I would go into stores that sold threads. One can't imagine how many thousands of reds there are. Spools in boxes lined up. You'd open a box that had pink written on it, and hundreds of different pinks would pour out!

EF: How can you even decide? The differences are so subtle, between a tacky pink and one that works, for some reason.

CK: I would try not to decide in the thread store. I would buy everything, and bring it back and play with it. When you put different shades of a color together, it produces an effect that is a lot different than just one. Then you go for the less shocking one. I am never looking for something shocking, but for something subtle. Shades of color take it down a step.

EF: Like in an Albers painting — different shades, depending on the size of the squares.

CK: I am also thinking about Agnes Martin. This takes me to Dia at Beacon.

EF: The Robert Ryman paintings.

CK: There's a room of them. It blew my mind. That was so exciting.

EF: A lot of times, seeing a group of an artist's work produces a very different impact than seeing only one.

CK: There was every shade of white possible. To me, it is so sophisticated.

EF: It's sublime. In this context, that word is not a cliché.

CK: I don't think about it in that way. At least, not as someone looking at paintings. People outside the art world are not thinking about it as a collective art world and what's in or what's out.

EF: I try not to also. That's one of the reasons I live out here. I need the separation.

CK: I think that's part of the reason artists and writers like it out here, in the Hamptons, because you can get your work done without interferences. As an outsider, I'm just looking for something that gets to me emotionally. Like those Robert Ryman paintings — they were very emotionally charged. And, I agree, the impact of seeing a group of them is quite incredible.

PLATES

The Art of Living, 2008

Oil on linen

91,5 x 183 cm (each panel: 91,5 x 91,5 cm)

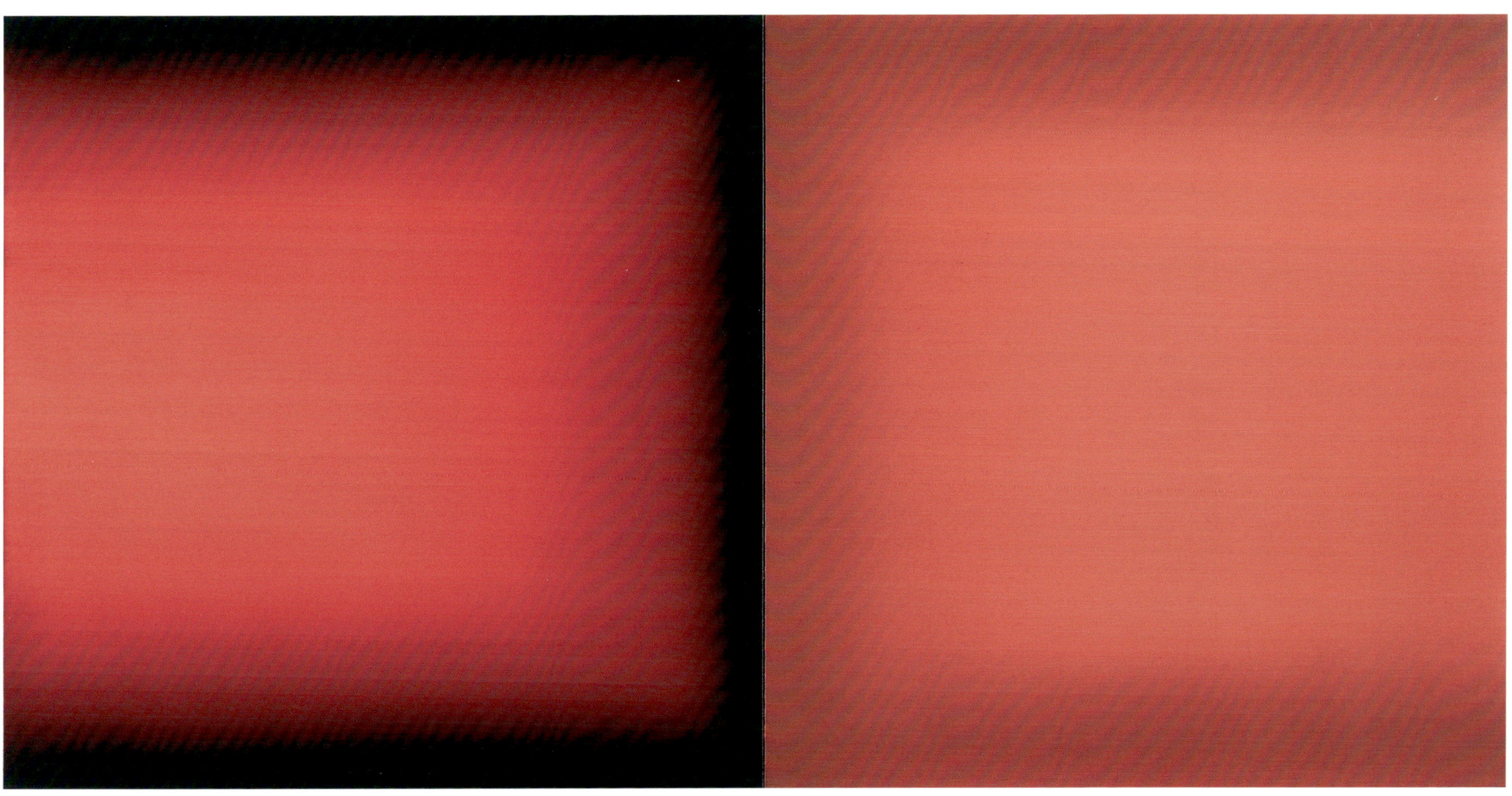

Truer Than History, 2008

Oil on linen

122 x 122 cm

Untitled for Alain Noirhomme, 2008

Oil on linen

122 x 122 cm

Rising Corridor, 2008

Oil on linen

122 x 122 cm

Indicator, 2008

Oil on linen

183 x 183 cm

Untitled for Claudia Cohen, 2007

Oil on linen

183 x 183 cm

Twisted, 2007

Oil on linen

183 x 213 cm

Ocean, 2007

Oil on linen

183 x 183 cm

Bench, 2008

natural white rubber and marine fir plywood

46 x 99 x 41 cm

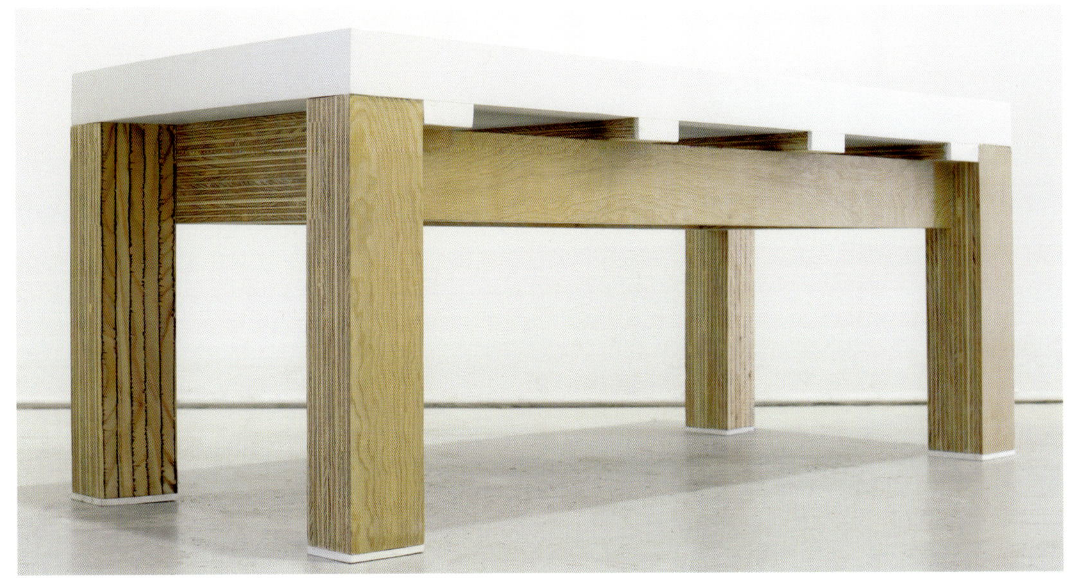

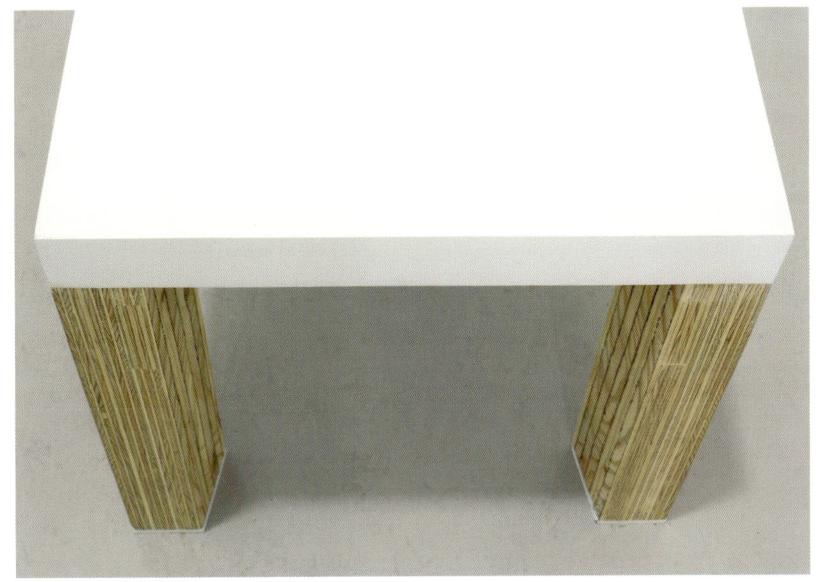

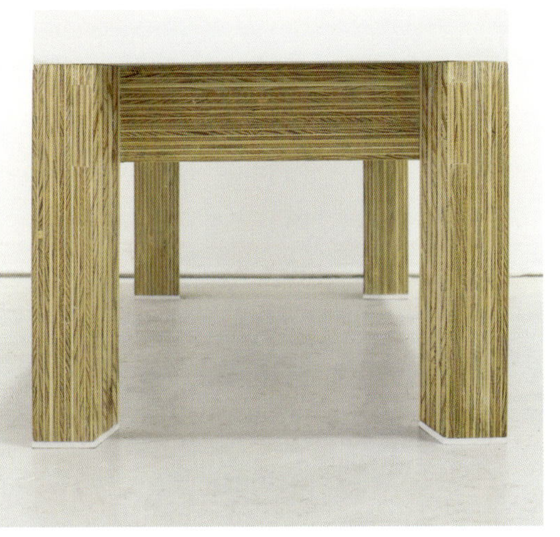

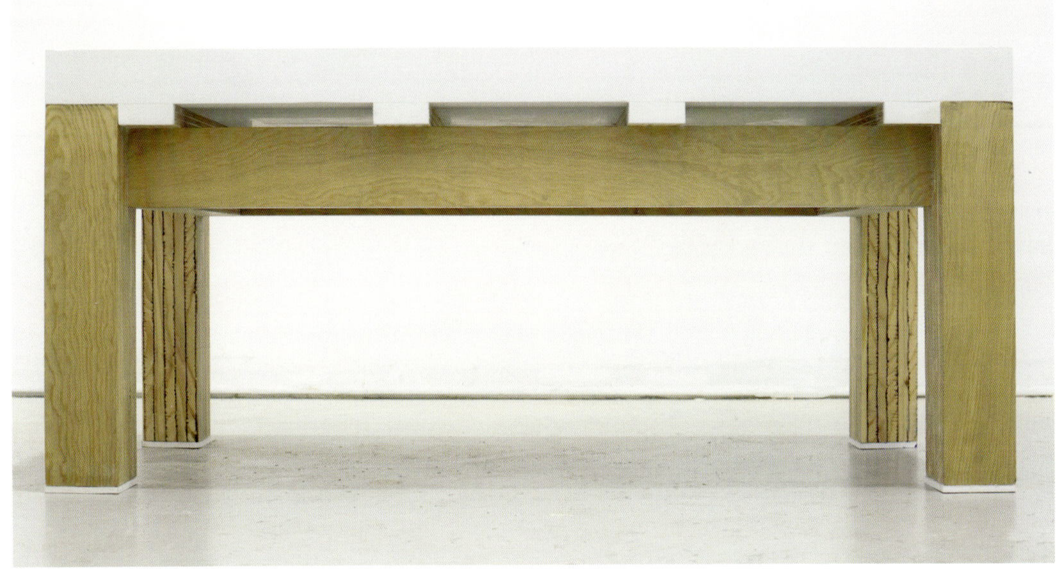

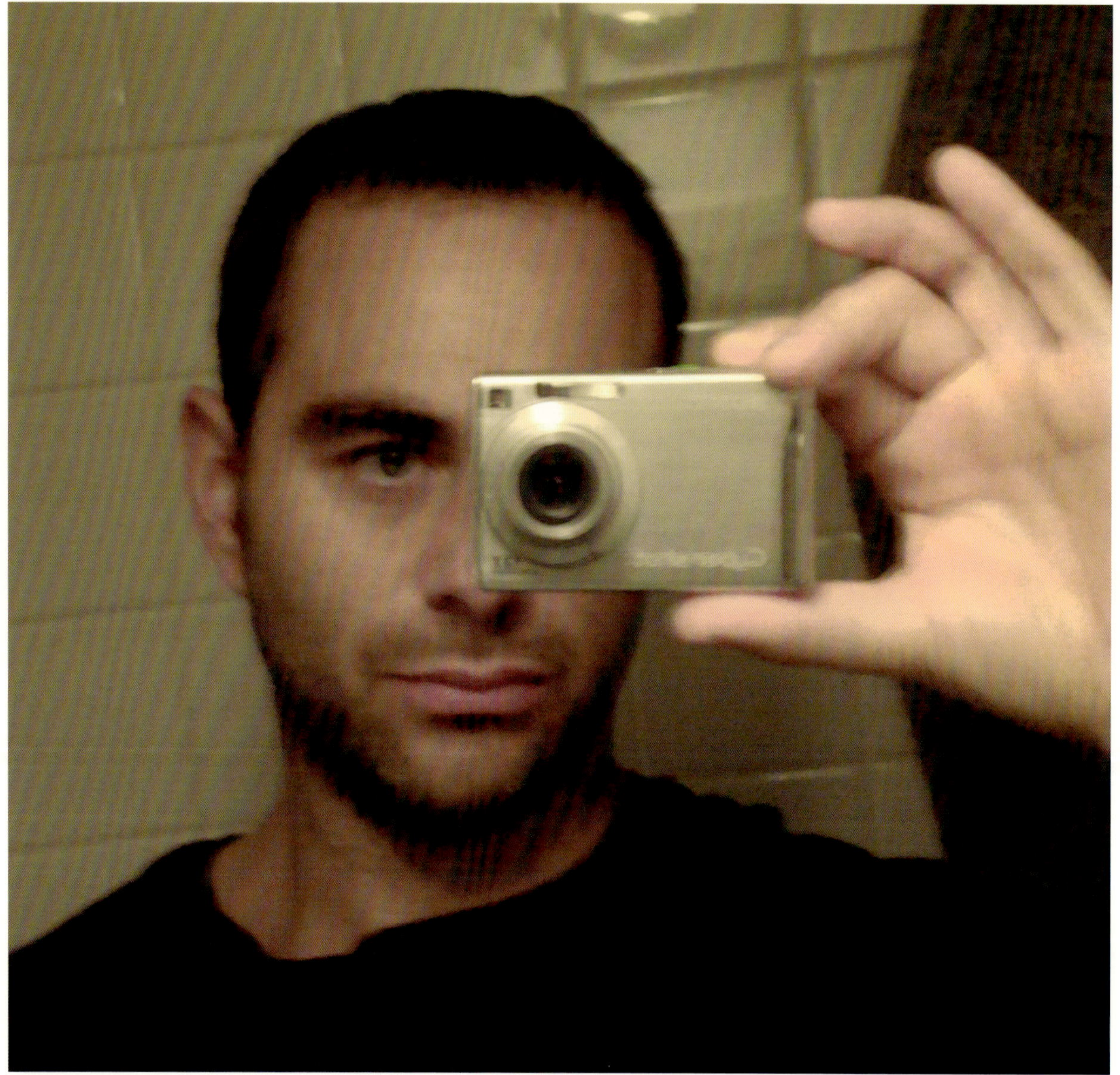

Eric Freeman

Photography by Eric Freeman

BIOGRAPHY

ERIC FREEMAN

Born in Brooklyn, New York, 1970
Lives in New York City and Sagaponack, New York

EDUCATION

Tufts University, Medford, Massachusetts, B.F.A., 1993

SELECTED SOLO SHOWS

2008   Alain Noirhomme Gallery, Brussels, Belgium
2007   Western-Project, Los Angeles, USA
2006   Galerie Forsblom, Helsinki, Finland
2005   Mary Boone Gallery, NYC, NY, USA
2004   Western Project, Culver City, California, USA
2003   Glenn Horowitz Booksellers Gallery, East Hampton, New York, USA
        Mark Moore Gallery, Los Angeles, California, USA
        Mary Boone Gallery, NYC, NY, USA
        Bjorn Wetterling Gallery, Stockholm, Sweden
2002   Mark Moore Gallery, Los Angeles, California, USA
2001   Stefan Stux Gallery, NYC, NY, USA
2000   Stefan Stux Gallery, NYC, NY, USA
1999   Gallery 56, Budapest, Hungary

SELECTED GROUP SHOWS

2008   Abstract America, The Saatchi Gallery, London, England
2006   Triumph of Painting, The Saatchi Gallery, London, England
2003   Glenn Horowitz Booksellers, East Hampton, New York, USA
2002   Glenn Horowitz Booksellers, East Hampton, New York, USA
2000   24/7, Guild Hall Museum, East Hampton, New York, USA
1997   The Moderns, Feature Gallery, NYC, NY, USA

SELECTED BIOGRAPHY

Mason, Brook S., Retro Fit Retro Modern, ART & ANTIQUES, September 2005, pp. 62-69.
Myers, Holly, Around the Galleries: Hard to look at, yet absorbing, LOS ANGELES TIMES, 24 December 2004.
Leffingwell, Edward, Eric Freeman at Mary Boone, ART IN AMERICA, September 2003, pp. 118-119.
Volandes, Stellene, Black Book: Patrick Mc Carthy, DEPARTURES, September 2003, p. 52.
Johnson, Ken, Eric Freeman, THE NEW YORK TIMES, 30 May 2003, p. E37.
Colacello, Bob, Eric Freeman, INTERVIEW, May 2003, p. 64.
Staff, Fanfair: May, VANITY FAIR, May 2003, p. 92.
Edelson, Sharon, WOMEN'S WEAR DAILY, 27 January 2003, p. 2.
Norwich, William, A.I.R. Rights, THE NEW YORK TIMES MAGAZINE, 30 June 2002, pp. 43-48.

ERIC FREEMAN

Catalogue and exhibition
Gallery Alain Noirhomme
Copyright © June, 2008

Photographs of the artist by Fred Torres

Photographs of the paintings by Oote Boe

Printed by
Graphic Production Cassochrome
Color Service Center

Books and catalogues available through
Editions Alain Noirhomme
Rue de la Régence 17 Regentschapsstraat
B-1000 Brussels
Tel 32 2 512 50 10   Fax 32 2 512 11 15
e-mail: lotus@skynet.be
www.alain-noirhomme.com

ISBN: 978-2-930487-05-2